Narrow Road to the Interior

NARROW ROAD
TO THE INTERIOR

Matsuo Bashō

Translated by Sam Hamill

Illustrated by Stephen Addiss

SHAMBHALA
Boston & London
1991

Shambhala Publications, Inc.
Horticultural Hall
300 Massachusetts Avenue
Boston, Massachusetts 02115

Shambhala Publications, Inc.
Random Century House
20 Vauxhall Bridge Road
London SW1V 2SA

9   8   7   6   5   4   3   2   1

First Edition
Printed in South Korea on acid-free paper
Distributed in the United States by Random House, Inc., in Canada by
Random House of Canada, Ltd, and in the United Kingdom by the
Random Century Group

Library of Congress Cataloging-in-Publication Data

Matsuo, Bashō, 1644–1694.
    [Oku no hosomichi. English]
    Narrow road to the interior/Matsuo Bashō; translated by Sam Hamill.—1st ed.
        p.   cm. — (Shambhala centaur editions)
    Translation of: Oku no hosomichi.
    1. Matsuo, Bashō, 1644–1694—Journeys—Japan. 2. Japan—
    ISBN 0-87773-644-8 (pbk.)
    Description and travel—To 1868. 3. Authors, Japanese—Edo period,
    1600–1868—Journeys—Japan. I. Hamill, Sam. II. Title. III. Series.
    PL794.4.Z5A3613   1991   91-8574
    895.6'132—dc20   CIP

To Kannon

Contents

Acknowledgments

I would like to express my sincere thanks to my friend and translator, Yusuke Keida, and to Burton Watson and John Solt, for valuable corrections and commentaries on my translation. Thanks are also due to my editor, Peter Turner, for his sensitive and helpful reading.

Translator's Introduction

DURING THE SPRING AND SUMMER OF 1689, the poet Bashō, accompanied by his friend Sora, walked the roads of Japan's Northern Interior, recording with almost complete detachment the essential and transient nature of the people and places encountered along the way. Between 1690 and 1694, he polished the little travel diary of that journey, and the result, *Oku-no-hosomichi*, translated here as *Narrow Road to the Interior*, is one of the most revered books in all of Japanese literature.

Oku means "within" and "farthest" or "dead-end" place; it also means "interior" both in the sense of interior country and spiritual interior. *No* is a possessive and is prepositional. *Hosomichi* means "path" or "trail" or "narrow road." *Oku-no-hosomichi* can then be taken to mean both a narrow road through the country's mountainous interior lying between Miyagino and Matsushima, and the metaphoric narrow trail leading into one's spiritual center.

Bashō's little book is not a true travel journal. The heart and soul of his masterpiece—its *kokoro*—arises out of strenuous studies in poetry and history, Buddhism, Taoism, Confucianism, Shinto traditions, and some intense personal Zen discipline. The publication of Sora's travel notes fifty years ago reveals that Bashō's claim to have visited some places and done some things may have been fictitious. Along most of the journey, for instance, Bashō and Sora were welcomed by wealthy merchant-class patrons. But Bashō describes a much more Spartan existence. These inventions serve a useful purpose within the context of the whole book, indicating Bashō's deep faith in his art as a poet and spiritual seeker. The fact that he worked on his book over the four years following the journey indicates that he wanted the work to stand apart from any literal reading of his adventure, emphasizing spiritual over auto-biographical qualities in the book. He did not, however, exaggerate his poor health and the very real physical dangers of the journey. Even though his journey took place during the Genroku period, a time of relative peace under the Tokugawa shogunate, travel was always dangerous. Bashō and Sora, like many others, dressed as Buddhist monks in part to ensure their safety.

In his mid-forties and in chronic poor health, Bashō was hardly an ideal candidate to walk the trails of the Northern Interior, even though he had already walked the roads of most of southern Honshu (the main island of Japan). One of the most renowned poets in a society that revered poetry, he found himself surrounded by followers at his little home along the banks of the Sumida River in present-day Tokyo, then called Edo. An admirer had planted a *bashō*, or plantain tree, near the house, and soon both the house and poet gained a new name.

Born Matsuo Munefusa in 1644 in the Iga Province village of Ueno, thirty miles southeast of Kyoto, Bashō served in his childhood as a companion to Yoshitada, the son of a local feudal lord, until his death in 1666. Both the death of his master and his own complicated love life—he may have been involved with ladies of the court, he had a common-law wife, and he also claimed to have become "fascinated with the ways of homosexual love"—left him ill-prepared for life as a samurai. He settled in Edo and for the next fifteen years wrote *renga* (linked verse) and haiku, living on patronage and building his reputation as a poet and teacher. In the winter of 1680, when several of his disciples built the hut that lent the poet his final nom de plume, he wrote:

Near the brushwood gate   *Shiba no to ni*
furious tea leaves scribble   *cha o konoha kaku*
nothings on the storm   *arashi kana*

The poem suggests a sense of elemental loneliness, as though the poet lived in some far wilderness rather than at the edge of a bustling, burgeoning city, and it leaves an aftertaste of *sabi*, a word that comes from *sabishisa*, loneliness. But *sabi* means far more than mere "loneliness" as we think of it: it means essential aloneness. In Zen, *sabi* is a condition of utter individuation achieved through solitary, egoless meditation. There is no ego in the poem. No one's there. The reader must project him- or herself into the flow of language and image in order to *experience* the poetry firsthand.

Modern Japanese poets often remark, "Haiku began and ended with Bashō." He had taken an essentially playful form and brought to it his profound Zen training and enormous literary scholarship, an ear for sound that was nonpareil, and a sweeping sense of the Way of Elegance (*fuga-no-michi*). In this poem even the non-Japanese reader can hear the *ah, o,* and *k* sounds, the *shi, ni, shi* sounds, the whole possessed of remarkable wind-in-tea-plant noises.

He had rejected bourgeois society and immersed himself in early Japanese and Chinese literature, especially the poetry of the Tang-dynasty poet Tu Fu, the twelfth-century Japanese Buddhist priest Saigyō, and the Taoist sage Chuang Tzu. Even greater than his elevation of haiku from mere literary play to the expression of profound Zen, his *haibun* (brief prose combined with haiku) established Bashō as one of the preeminent figures in all of Japanese literature. His *haibun*, especially *Oku-no-hosomichi*, relies very heavily on a literary tradition called *honkadori*, allusive poems, even revisions of poems, "answers" to poems from the classics. There is hardly a phrase in *Oku-no-hosomichi* that is not loaded with allusion, resonance, quotation, or paraphrase from Chuang Tzu, Tu Fu, Li Po, Saigyō, Kamo-no-Chōmei, the epic *Tale of Genji*, and other sources. He wrote for a highly literate, highly sophisticated audience.

By 1689, success weighed heavily on the poet. Students and sycophants alike visited constantly. He was deeply interested in the "return to original mind" (*honshin*) encouraged in Zen training; that is, he longed to find his own deepest personal connection to the very real world that lay only far beyond adoring crowds and poetry-writing contests. The fundamental teaching of Buddhism is codependent origination—that nothing is entirely self-originating. Bashō's journey would be a return to the elemental world, a return to natural, spiritual, and literary origins.

He clearly felt that social obligations interfered with his spiritual growth, and that spiritual growth was, after all, the wellspring of his verse and his life as an artist. Perhaps he was merely undergoing what our culture terms "midlife crisis." He felt nonetheless a desperate need to experience a rebirth both as an artist and as a Zennist, and it is no small testimony to his devotion to Zen practice and to his modesty as an artist that he would seek a major personal transformation at the very pinnacle of popular success.

Bashō knew well the *Samantabhadra-bodhisattva-sutra* and its primary teaching: "Of one thing it is said, 'This is good,' and of another it is said,

'This is bad,' but there is nothing inherent in either to make them 'good' or 'bad.' The 'self' is empty of independent existence." Dreaming of the full moon rising over fishing boats and tiny pine islands at Matsushima, Bashō is not looking outside himself, but rather locating "meaning" within the context of juxtaposed images that are interpenetrating and interdependent. The images themselves, true to Chinese literary Zen pedagogy, arise naturally out of the *hsin* (Japanese: *kokoro*), the heart-soul-mind of the poet. The self is empty of independent existence.

But the self, especially in the case of Bashō, is not empty of personality. The poet is not the least embarrassed by moments of sentimentality, apprehension, or outright fear, and his sense of profound irony is in good working order. For example, upon seeing the magisterial "jeweled Buddha-land" of Zuigan Temple, he suddenly longs to visit the tiny, simple temple hermitage of the mendicant priest Kembutsu; and again when he remarks about remote Eihei Temple that its location "a thousand miles from the capital" is no accident. In the midst of a terrible storm high in a mountain pass, he notes with humor and frustration the horse that spatters his pillow with piss. Unable to lead the way for a couple of young prostitutes on a pilgrimage, he later feels some regret.

Having learned from Saigyō, Kamo-no-Chōmei, and other Zen poets that seer and seen are not two things but one, Bashō remains a not-entirely-detached, compassionate participant as well as an observer. In his practice, he follows the teaching of the ninth-century

Chinese Zen master Te-shan, "No mind in work, no work in mind," which directs the Zennist to be free of all self-consciousness, to be *buji*, completely free of anxiety. While working, work; while resting, rest. Bashō had often told his own students, "Learn the rules well, and then forget them," his instruction echoing that of Zen master Yun-men (864–949), "When a great act presents itself, it does so without rules."

In the spring of 1689, the famous cherry trees of Ueno and Yanaka in splendid bloom, Bashō prepared to follow the *oku-no-hosomichi* across the Shirakawa Barrier into the heart of northern Honshu, visiting famous literary sites along the way, often ignoring other, equally or even more breathtaking views, writing brief prose passages and some haiku that would connect him forever to the world's literature of travel and to the Zen tradition. He had prepared himself to meet the great act. He patched his cotton trousers, repaired his straw hat, shouldered his pack, and began a long journey into the soul's interior.

Narrow Road to the Interior

THE MOON AND SUN are eternal travelers. Even the years wander on. A lifetime adrift in a boat, or in old age leading a tired horse into the years, every day is a journey, and the journey itself is home. From the earliest times there have always been some who perished along the road. Still I have always been drawn by windblown clouds into dreams of a lifetime of wandering. Coming home from a year's walking tour of the coast last autumn, I swept the cobwebs from my hut on the banks of the Sumida just in time for New Year, but by the time spring mists began to rise from the fields, I longed to cross the Shirakawa Barrier into the Northern Interior. Drawn by the wanderer-spirit Dōsojin, I couldn't concentrate on things. Mending my cotton pants, sewing a new strap on my bamboo hat, I daydreamed. Rubbing moxa into my legs to strengthen them, I dreamed a bright moon rising over Matsushima. So I placed my house in another's hands and moved to my patron Mr. Sampū's summer house in preparation for my journey. And I left a verse by my door:

> Even this grass hut
> may be transformed
> into a doll's house

VERY EARLY on the twenty-seventh morning of the third moon, under a predawn haze, transparent moon still visible, Mount Fuji just a shadow, I set out under the cherry blossoms of Ueno and Yanaka. When would I see them again? A few old friends had gathered in the night and followed along far enough to see me off from the boat. Getting off at Senju, I felt three thousand miles rushing through my heart, the whole world only a dream. I saw it through farewell tears.

> Spring passes
> and the birds cry out—
> tears in the eyes of fishes

With these first words from my brush, I started. Those who remain behind watch the shadow of a traveler's back disappear.

THE SECOND YEAR of Genroku [1689], I think of the long way leading into the Northern Interior under Go stone skies. My hair may turn white as frost before I return from those fabled places—or maybe I won't return at all. By nightfall, we come to Sōka, bony shoulders sore from heavy pack, grateful for warm night robe, cotton bathing gown, writing brush, ink stone, necessities. The pack made heavier by farewell gifts from friends. I couldn't leave them behind.

CONTINUING ON to the shrine at Muro-no-Yashima, my companion Sora said, "This deity, Ko-no-hana Sakuya Hime, is Goddess of Blossoming Trees and also has a shrine at Fuji. She locked herself inside a fire to prove her son's divinity. Thus her son was called Prince Hohodemi—Born-of-Fire—here in Muro-no-Yashima (Burning Cell). And that's why poets here write of smoke, and why the locals despise the splotched *konoshiro* fish that reeks like burning flesh. Everyone here knows the story."

THE LAST NIGHT of the third moon, an inn at the foot of Mount Nikkō. The innkeeper is called Hoteke Gozaemon—Joe Buddha. He says his honesty earned him the name and invites me to make myself at home. A merciful buddha like an ordinary man, he suddenly appeared to help a pilgrim along his way. His simplicity's a great gift, his sincerity unaffected. A model of Confucian rectitude, my host is a saint.

ON THE FIRST DAY of the fourth moon, climbed to visit the shrines on a mountain once called Two Wildernesses, renamed by Kūkai when he dedicated the shrine. Perhaps he saw a thousand years into the future, this shrine under sacred skies, his compassion endlessly scattered through the eight directions, falling equally, peaceably, on all four classes of people. The greater the glory, the less these words can say.

Speechless before
these budding green spring leaves
in blazing sunlight

MOUNT KUROKAMI still clothed in snow, faint in the mist, Sora wrote:

> Head shaven
> at Black Hair Mountain
> we change into summer clothes

Sora was named Kawai Sōgorō; Sora's his nom de plume. At my old home—called Bashō (plantain tree)—he carried water and wood. Anticipating the pleasures of seeing Matsushima and Kisagata, we agreed to share the journey, pleasure and hardship alike. The morning we started, he put on Buddhist robes, shaved his head, and changed his name to Sogo, the Enlightened. So the "changing clothes" in his poem is pregnant with meaning.

A hundred yards uphill, the waterfall plunged a hundred feet from its cavern in the ridge, falling into a basin made by a thousand stones. Crouched in the cavern behind the falls, looking out, I understood why it's called Urami-no-Taki, "View-from-behind-Falls."

Stopped awhile
inside a waterfall:
the summer begins

A FRIEND LIVES IN KUROBANE on the far side of the broad Nasu Moor. Tried a shortcut running straight through, but it began to rain in the early evening, so we stopped for the night at a village farmhouse and continued again at dawn. Out in the field, a horse, and nearby a man cutting grass. I stopped to ask directions. Courteous, he thought awhile, then said, "Too many intersecting roads. It's easy to get lost. Best to take that old horse as far as he'll go. He knows the road. When he stops, get off, and he'll come back alone."

Two small children danced along behind, one with the curious name of Kasane, same as the pink flower. Sora wrote:

> With this *kasane*
> she's doubly pink
> a fitting name

Arriving at a village, I tied a small gift to the saddle and the horse turned back.

ONCE IN KUROBANE, I visited the powerful samurai Jōbōji, overseer of the manor. Surprised by the visit, he kept me up talking through several days and nights, often at the home of his brother Tōsui. We visited their relatives and friends. One day we walked out to Inu oumono, Dog-shooting Grounds. We walked out into the moors to find the tomb of Lady Tamamo, who turned herself to stone. We paid homage at Hachiman Shrine, where Yoshitsune's general Yoichi shot a fan from a passing boat after praying to Shō-hachiman, warrior-god of this shrine. At dusk we returned to Tōsui's home.

Invited to visit Shūgen Kōmyō Temple's hall for mountain monks:

> In summer mountains
> bow to holy high water clogs
> bless this long journey

IN A MOUNTAIN HERMITAGE near Ungan Temple, my dharma master Butchō wrote:

> A five-foot thatched hut:
> I wouldn't even put it up
> but for the falling rain

He inscribed the poem on a rock with charcoal—he told me long ago. Curious, several young people joined in, walking sticks pointed toward Ungan Temple. We were so caught up in talking we arrived at the temple unexpectedly. Through the long valley, under dense cedar and pine with dripping moss, below a cold spring sky—through the viewing gardens, we crossed a bridge and entered the temple gate.

I searched out back for Butchō's hermitage and found it up the hill, near a cave on a rocky ridge—like the cave where Myōzenji lived for fifteen years, like Zen master Hōun's retreat.

> Even woodpeckers leave it alone:
> a hermitage
> in a summer grove

One small poem, quickly written, pinned to a post.

SET OUT TO SEE the Murder Stone, Sesshō-seki, on a borrowed horse, and the man leading it asked for a poem, "Something beautiful, please."

> The horse lifts his head:
> from across deep fields
> the cuckoo's cry

Sesshō-seki lies in dark mountain shadow near a hot springs emitting bad gases. Dead bees and butterflies cover the sand.

AT ASHINO, the willow Saigyō praised, "beside the crystal stream," still grows along a path in fields of rice. A local official had offered to lead the way, and I had often wondered whether and where it remained. And now, today, that same willow:

> Girls' rice-planting done
> they depart:
> I emerge from willow-shade

A LITTLE ANXIOUS, thinking of the Shirakawa Barrier, thinking on it day by day, but calmed my mind by remembering the old poem, "somehow sending word home." I walked through heavy green summer forests. Many a poet inscribed a few words at one of the Three Barriers—"autumn winds" and "red maple leaves" come to mind. Then, like fields of snow, innumerable white-flowered bushes, *unohana*, covered either side of the road. Here, Kiyosuke wrote, people dressed their very best to pass through the mountain gate, men in small black formal hats as though dressed for the highest courts. Sora wrote:

> *Unohana*
> around my head
> dressed for ancient rites

OVER THE PASS, we crossed the Abukuma River, Mount Aizu to the left, the villages of Iwaki, Sōma, and Miharu on the right, divided from the villages of Hitachi and Shimotsuke by two small mountain ranges. At Kagenuma, the Mirror Pond, a dark sky blurred every reflection.

We spent several days in Sukagawa with the poet Tōkyū, who asked about the Shirakawa Barrier. "With mind and body sorely tested," I answered, "busy with other poets' lines, engaged in splendid scenery, it's hardly surprising I didn't write much":

> Culture's beginnings:
> from the heart of the country
> rice-planting songs

"From this opening verse," I told him, "we wrote three linked-verse poems."

IN THE SHADE of a huge chestnut at the edge of town, a monk made his hermitage a refuge from the world. Saigyō's poem about gathering chestnuts deep in the mountains refers to such a place. I wrote on a slip of paper: The Chinese character for *chestnut* means "west tree," alluding to the Western Paradise of Amida Buddha; the priest Gyōki, all his life, used chestnut for his walking stick and for the posts of his home.

> Near the eaves
> the chestnut blooms:
> almost no one sees

WALKED A FEW MILES from Tōkyū's home to the town of Hiwada in the foothills of Mount Asaka. Marshlands glistened outside of town. Almost midsummer, iris-picking time. I asked about blossoming *katsumi*, but no one knew where they grew. I searched all day, muttering, *"Katsumi, katsumi,"* until the sun set over the mountains.

We followed a road to the right at Nihonmatsu and stopped to see Kurozuka Cave. And stayed the night in Fukushima.

At DAWN we left for Shinobu, famous for dyed cloth—called *shinobu-zuri*—named after the rock we found half buried in the mountain. Village children joined us and explained, "In the old days, the rock was on top of the mountain, but visitors trampled farmers' crops, so the old men rolled it down." Their story made perfect sense.

> Girls' busy hands plant rice
> almost like
> the ancient ones making dye

CROSSED ON THE FERRY at Tsukinowa to the post town of Se-no-ue to see the ruins that were Satō Shōji's house, beyond town to the left, near the mountains. We were told to look at Saba Moor in Iizuka, and we eventually came to Maru Hill, where the castle ruins lay. Seeing the main gate sundered, the ancient temple nearby, seeing all the family graves, tears glazed my eyes. Especially at the tombs of two young widows who had dressed in the armor of fallen sons and then lay down their lives. Like Tu Yu at Weeping Gravemound, I dried my eyes with a sleeve. Inside the temple, enjoying tea, Yoshitsune's great long sword and the priest Benkei's little Buddhist wicker chest, both enshrined:

Sword, chest, and wind-carp
all proudly displayed
on Boys' Festival Day

It was the first of Satsuki, rice-planting month.

STAYING THE NIGHT in Iizuka, we bathed in a mineral hot springs before returning to thin straw sleeping mats on bare ground—a true country inn. Without a lamp, we made our beds by firelight, in flickering shadows, and closed our tired eyes. Suddenly a thunderous downpour and leaky roof aroused us, fleas and mosquitoes everywhere. Old infirmities tortured me throughout the long, sleepless night.

At first light, long before dawn, we packed our things and left, distracted, tired, but moving on. Sick and worried, we hired horses to ride to the town of Kori. I worried about my plans. With every pilgrimage one encounters the temporality of life. To die along the road is destiny. Or so I told myself. I stiffened my will and, once resolute, crossed Ōkido Barrier in Date Province.

THROUGH narrow Abumizuri Pass and on, passing Shiroishi Castle, we entered Kasashima Province. We asked for directions to the gravemound of Lord Sanekata, Sei Shonagon's exiled poet-lover, and were told to turn right on the hills near the villages of Minowa and Kasashima when we came to the Shrine of Dōsojin. It lies nearly hidden in sedge grass Saigyō remembered in a poem. May rains turned the trail to mud. We stopped, sick and worn out, and looked at the two aptly named villages in the distance: Straw Raincoat Village and Umbrella Island.

> Where's Kasashima?
> Lost on a muddy road
> in the rainy season

The night was spent in Iwanuma.

DEEPLY TOUCHED by the famous pine at Takekuma, twin trunks just as long ago. The poet-priest Nōin came to mind. Before he came, Lord Fujiwara-no-Takayoshi cut down the tree for lumber, building a bridge across the Natorigawa. Nōin wrote: "No sign here now of that famous pine." Reported to have been cut down and replaced several times, it stood like a relic of a thousand years, impossibly perfect. The poet Kyohaku had given me a poem at my departure:

> Remember to show my master
> the famous Takekuma pine,
> O northern blossoming cherries

To which I now reply:

Ever since cherry blossom time
I longed to visit two-trunked pine:
three long months have passed

WE CROSSED OVER the Natorigawa on the seventh day, fifth moon, and entered Sendai on the day we tie blue iris to the eaves and pray for health. We found an inn and decided to spend several days. I'd heard of a painter here, Kaemon, who was a kindred spirit and had visited all the nearby places the poets had made famous. Before him, these places were all but forgotten. He agreed to be our guide. The fields at Miyagi were carpeted with bush clover that would bloom in autumn. In Tamada and Yokono and at Azalea Hill there were andromeda flowers in bloom. Passing through pine woods sunlight couldn't penetrate, we came to Kinoshita, the "Under Woods" where the poet in the *Kokinshū* begged an umbrella for his lord in falling dew. We visited Yakushido Shrine and the Shrine of Tenjin until the sun went down.

Later the painter gave us drawings of Matsushima and Shiogama. And two pairs of new straw sandals with iris-blue straps—*hanamuke*, farewell gifts. He was a truly kindred spirit.

> To have blue irises
> blooming on one's feet:
> walking-sandal straps

CHECKING KAEMON's drawings as we walked, we followed the *oku-no-hosomichi* along the mountainside where sedge grass grew tall in bunches. The Tofu area is famous for its sedge mats, sent in tribute to the governor each year.

At Taga Castle we found the most ancient monument Tsubo-no-ishibumi, in Ichikawa Village. It's about six feet high and three feet wide. We struggled to read the inscription under heavy moss:

> This Castle was Built by Shogun Ono-no-Azumabito in 724. In 762, His Majesty's Commanding General, Emi-no-Asakari, Supervised Repairs.

Dated from the time of Emperor Shōmu, Tsubo-no-ishibumi inspired many a poet. Floods and landslides buried trails and markers, trees have grown and died, making this monument very difficult to find. The past remains hidden in clouds of memory. Still it returned us to memories from a thousand years before. Such a moment is the reason for a pilgrimage: infirmities forgotten, the ancients remembered, joyous tears trembled in my eyes.

WE STOPPED along the Tama River at Noda, and at the huge stone in the lake, Oki-no-ishi, both made famous in poems. On Mount Sue-no-matsu, we found a temple called Masshozan. There were graves everywhere among the pines, underscoring Po Chu-i's famous lines quoted in *The Tale of Genji*, "wing and wing, branch and branch," and I thought, "Yes, what we all must come to," my sadness heavy.

At Shiogama Beach, a bell sounded evening. The summer rain-sky cleared to reveal a pale moon high over Magaki Island. I remembered the "fishing boats pulling together" in a *Kokinshū* poem, and understood it clearly for the first time.

> Along the Michinoku
> every place is wonderful,
> but in Shiogama

> fishing boats pulling together
> are most amazing of all

That night we were entertained by a blind singer playing a lute to boisterous back-country ballads one hears only deep inside the country, not like the songs in *The Tale of the Heike* or the dance songs. A real earful, but pleased to hear the tradition continued.

Rose at dawn to pay respects at Myōjin Shrine in Shiogama. The former governor rebuilt it with huge, stately pillars, bright-painted rafters, and a long stone walkway rising steeply under a morning sun that danced and flashed along the red lacquered fence. I thought, "As long as the road is, even if it ends in dust, the gods come with us, keeping a watchful eye. This is our culture's greatest gift." Kneeling at the shrine, I noticed a fine old lantern with this inscribed on its iron grate:

In the Third Year of the Bunji Era [1187]
Dedicated by Izumi Saburō

Suddenly, five long centuries passed before my eyes. A trusted, loyal man martyred by his brother; today there's not a man alive who doesn't revere his name. As he himself would

say, a man must follow the Confucian model—
renown will inevitably result.

SUN HIGH OVERHEAD before we left the shrine, we hired a boat to cross to Matsushima, a mile or more away. We disembarked on Ojima Beach.

As many others often observed, the views of Matsushima take one's breath away. It may be—along with Lake Tung-t'ing and West Lake in China—the most beautiful place in the world. Islands in a three-mile bay, the sea to the southeast entering like floodtide on the Ch'ien-t'ang River in Chekiang. Small islands, tall islands pointing at the sky, islands on top of islands, islands like mothers with baby islands on their backs, islands cradling islands in the bay. All covered with deep green pines shaped by salty winds, trained into sea-wind bonsai. Here one is almost overcome by the sense of intense feminine beauty in a shining world. It must have been the mountain god Ōyamazumi who made this place. And whose words or brush could adequately describe a world so divinely inspired?

OJIMA BEACH is not—as its name implies—
an island, but a strand projected into the bay.
Here one finds the ruins of Ungo Zenji's
hermitage and the rock where he sat *zazen*. And
still a few tiny thatched huts under pines where
religious hermits live in tranquillity. Smoke of
burning leaves and pine cones drew me on,
touching something deep inside. Then the
moon rose, shining on the sea, day turned
suddenly to night. We stayed at an inn on the
shore, our second-story windows opening on
the bay. Drifting with winds and clouds, it was
almost like a dream. Sora wrote:

> In Matsushima
> you'll need the wings of a crane
> little cuckoo

I was speechless and tried to sleep, but rose to dig from my pack a Chinese-style poem my friend Sodō had written for me, something about Pine Islands. And also a *waka* by Hara Anteki, and haiku by Sampu and Dakushi.

O N THE ELEVENTH DAY, fifth moon, we visited Zuigan Temple and were met by the thirty-second-generation descendant of the founder. Established by Makabe-no-Heishiro at the time he returned from religious studies in T'ang China, the temple was enlarged under Ungo Zenji into seven main structures with new blue tile roofs, walls of gold, a jeweled Buddha-land. But my mind wandered, wondering if the priest Kembutsu's tiny temple might be found.

Early morning of the twelfth day, fifth moon. We started out for Hiraizumi, intending to go by way of the famous Aneha Pine and the Odae Bridge. The trail was narrow and little-traveled—only the occasional woodcutter or hunter. We took a wrong road and ended up in the port town of Ishinomaki on a broad bay with Mount Kinka in the distance. Yakamochi has a poem for the emperor in the *Man'yōshū* saying Kinka's "where gold blossoms." It rises across water cluttered with cargo boats and fishing boats, shoreline packed with houses, smoke rising from their stoves. Our unplanned visit prompted an immediate search for lodging. No one made an offer. Spent the night in a cold shack and left again at daybreak, following unknown paths. We passed near the Sode Ferry, Obuchi Meadow, and the Mano

Moor—all made famous in poems. After crossing a long miserable marsh, we stayed at Toima, pushing on to Hiraizumi in the morning. An arduous trek of over forty difficult miles in two days.

HERE THREE GENERATIONS of the Fujiwara clan passed as though in a dream. The great outer gates lay in ruins. Where Hidehira's manor stood, rice fields grew. Only Mount Kinkei remained. I climbed the hill where Yoshitsune died; I saw the Kitakami, a broad stream flowing down through the Nambu Plain, the Koromo River circling Izumi Castle below the hill before joining the Kitakami. The ancient ruins of Yasuhira—from the end of the Golden Era—lie out beyond the Koromo Barrier where they stood guard against the Ainu people. The faithful elite remained bound to the castle, for all their valor, reduced to ordinary grass. Tu Fu wrote:

> The whole country devastated,
> only mountains and rivers remain.

> In springtime, at the ruined castle,
> the grass is always green.

We sat awhile, our hats for a seat, seeing it all through tears.

> Summer grasses:
> all that remains of great soldiers'
> imperial dreams

Sora wrote:

> Kanefusa's
> own white hair
> seen in blossoming briar

TWO TEMPLE HALLS I longed to see were finally opened at Chuson Temple. In the Sutra Library, Kyōdō, statues of the three generals of Hiraizumi; and in the Hall of Light, Hikaridō, their coffins and images of three buddhas. It would have all fallen down, jeweled doors battered by winds, gold pillars cracked by cold, all would have gone to grass, but added outer roof and walls protect it. Through the endless winds and rains of a thousand years, this great hall remains.

> Fifth-month rains hammer
> and blow but never quite touch
> Hikaridō

THE ROAD through the Nambu Plain visible in the distance, we stayed the night in Iwate, then trudged on past Cape Oguro and Mizu Island, both along the river. Beyond Narugo Hot Springs, we crossed Shitomae Barrier and entered Dewa Province. Almost no one comes this way, and the barrier guards were suspicious, slow, and thorough. Delayed, we climbed a steep mountain in falling dark and took refuge in a guard shack. A heavy storm pounded the shack with wind and rain for three miserable days.

> Eaten alive by lice and fleas
> now the horse
> beside my pillow pees

THE GUARD told us, "To get to Dewa, you'd better take a guide. There's a high mountain and a hard-to-find trail." He found us a powerful young man, short sword on his hip and oak walking stick in hand, and off we went, not without a little trepidation. As forewarned, the mountain was steep, the trail narrow, not even a birdcall to be heard. We made our way through deep forest dark as night, reminding me of Tu Fu's poem about "clouds bringing darkness." We groped through thick bamboo, waded streams, climbed through rocks, sweaty, fearful, and tired, until we finally came to the village of Mogami. Our guide, turning back, said again how the trail was tough. "Happy you didn't meet many surprises!" And departed. Hearing this, our hearts skipped another beat.

Visited a merchant in Obanazawa, a Mr. Seifū, finding him to be wealthy but relatively free of the vulgarities of the merchant class. And he knew from his own many travels to Miyako the trials of life on the road, so invited us to stay the week. All in all, quite relaxing.

"My house is your house"
and so it is—cool,
sleeping in, sprawling out

Come out from hiding
under the silkworm room
little demon toad.

Little rouge brush
reminding me
of local safflower fields

Sora wrote:

> Women in the silkworm room
> all dressed simply
> like women in antiquity

IN YAMAGATA PROVINCE, the ancient temple founded by Jikaku Daishi in 860, Ryūshaku Temple, is stone quiet, perfectly tidy. Everyone told us to see it. It meant a few miles extra, doubling back toward Obanazawa to find shelter. Monks at the foot of the mountain offered rooms, then we climbed the ridge to the temple, scrambling up through ancient gnarled pine and oak, smooth gray stones and moss. The temple doors, built on rocks, were bolted. I crawled among boulders to make my bows at shrines. The silence was profound. I sat, feeling my heart begin to open.

> Lonely silence
> a single cicada's cry
> sinking into stone

PLANNING TO RIDE down the Mogami River, we were delayed at Ōishida, waiting for decent weather. "This is haiku country," someone told us, "seeds from old days blooming like forgotten flowers, the sound of a bamboo flute moving the heart. With no one to show us the way, however, local poets try new style and old style together." We made a small anthology together, but the result is of little merit. So much for culture.

The Mogami flows from the Michinoku at the far northern edge of Yamagata country. It is dangerous through Go Stone Rapids and Falcon Rapids, circumscribing northern Mount Itajiki to meet the sea at Sakata. Mountains rose from either side of the boat as we sped between the trees. The boat was only a tiny rice boat not meant for all we carried. We passed Shiraito Falls where it tumbles under pines. Sennin, Hall of Immortals, on the riverbank. The waters so high, it was a dangerous ride.

> All the summer rains
> violently gather:
> Mogami River

CLIMBED MOUNT HAGURO on the third day of the sixth moon and, with the help of a friend who dyes cloth for mountain monks' robes, Zushi Sakichi, obtained an audience with the abbott of Gongen Shrine, Master Egaku, who greeted us warmly. He arranged for quarters at nearby South Valley Temple. The next day we met at the main temple to write haiku:

> The winds that blow
> through South Valley Temple
> are sweetened by snow

WE PAID HOMAGE at Gongen Shrine on the fifth. The first shrine on the mountain, it was built by Nōjō, no one knows exactly when. The *Engi Ceremonies* calls it Ushusato Mountain, Feather Province Village Mountain, but calligraphers' errors got it changed to Feather *Black* Mountain. The province is called Dewa, Feather Tribute, dating from an eighth-century custom whereby feather-down from this region was used as payment of tribute. Together with Moon Mountain and Bath Mountain, Feather Black Mountain completes the Dewa Sanzan, or Three Holy Mountains of Dewa. This temple is Tendai sect, like the one in Edo on Toei Hill. Both follow the doctrine of *shikan*, "concentration and insight," a way of enlightenment as transparent as moonlight, its light infinitely increasing, spreading from hermitage to mountaintop and back, reverence and compassion shining in everything it touches. Its blessing flows down from these mountains, enriching all our lives.

On the eighth we climbed Moon Mountain, wearing the holy paper necklaces and cotton hats of Shinto priests, following behind a mountain monk whose footsteps passed through mist and clouds and snow and ice, climbing miles higher as though drawn by invisible spirits into the gateway of the sky— sun, moon, and clouds floated by and took my breath away. Long after sunset, moon high over the peak, we reached the summit, spread out in bamboo grass, and slept. Next day, after the sun burned away the clouds, we started down toward Yudono, Bath Mountain.

Approaching the valley, we passed Swordsmith Hut, named for the twelfth-century smith Gassan, who purified himself with holy water here and used it to temper his blades. On each blade he inscribed "Gassan," Moon

Mountain. He admired the famous Dragon Spring swords of China. I remembered the legendary man-and-wife smiths renowned for their dedication to detail and technique.

We stretched on a rock to rest and noticed the opening buds of a three-foot cherry tree. Buried under stubborn snow, it insists upon honoring spring, however late it arrives. Like the Chinese poem, "Plum blossoms fragrant in burning sun!" And Gyōson Sōjō wrote, "So sad, blossoming cherry, you have no one to admire you." It's all here, in these tiny blossoms!

To say more is sacrilege. Forbidden to speak, put down the brush, respect Shinto rites. Later, back with Master Egaku, we wrote poems on the Three Holy Mountains:

Cool crescent moon
high above
Feather Black Mountain

How many rising clouds
collapse and fall
on the Moon's Mountain

Forbidden to speak
alone on Yudono Mountain
tears on my sleeve

Sora wrote:

Bath Mountain walkway
paved with pilgrims' coins:
here too are tears

AFTER LEAVING HAGURO we came to the castle town of Tsuru-ga-oka accompanied by Zushi Sakichi and were greeted by the samurai Nagayama Shigeyuki. We composed a round of haiku, bade farewell, and started by boat down the Mogami, bound for Sakata Harbor. We stayed overnight with a certain doctor who wrote under the nom de plume En-an Fugyoku.

> From Hot Sea Mountain
> southward to Windy Beach
> the evening cools

> A burning summer sun
> slowly drowns:
> Mogami River

AFTER ALL the breathtaking views of rivers and mountains, lands and seas, after everything we'd seen, thoughts of seeing Kisakata's famous bay still made my heart begin to race. Twenty miles north of Sakata Harbor, as we walked the sandy shore beneath mountains where sea winds wander, a storm came up at dusk and covered Mount Chōkai in mist and rain reminiscent of Su Tung-p'o's famous poem. We made our way in the dark, hoping for a break in the weather, groping on until we found a fisherman's shack. By dawn the sky had cleared, sun dancing on the harbor. We took a boat for Kisakata, stopping by the priest Nōin's island retreat, honoring his three-year seclusion. On the opposite shore we saw the ancient cherry tree Saigyō saw reflected and immortalized, "Fishermen row over blossoms."

Near the shore, Empress Jingū's tomb. And Kammanju Temple. Did the empress ever visit? Why is she buried here?

Sitting in the temple chamber with the blinds raised, we saw the whole lagoon, Mount Chōkai holding up the heavens inverted on the water. To the west the road leads to the Muyamuya Barrier; to the east it curves along a bank toward Akita; to the north the sea comes in on tide flats at Shiogoshi. The whole lagoon, though only a mile or so across, reminds one of Matsushima, although Matsushima seems much more contented, whereas Kisakata seems bereaved. A sadness maybe in its sense of isolation here, where nature's darker spirits hide—like a strange and beautiful woman whose heart has been broken.

Kisakata rain
the legendary beauty Seishi
wrapped in sleeping leaves

At Shiogoshi
the long-legged crane
cool, stepping in the sea

Sora wrote:

Kisakata Festival:
at holy feasts
what specialties do locals eat?

The merchant Teiji from Mino Province wrote:

Fishermen sit
on their shutters on the sand
enjoying the evening cool

Sora found an osprey nest in the rocks:

> May the ocean resist
> violating the vows
> of the osprey's nest

After several days, clouds gathering over the North Road, we left Sakata reluctantly, aching at the thought of a hundred thirty miles to the provincial capital of Kaga. We crossed the Nezu Barrier into Echigo Province, and from there went on to Ichiburi Barrier in Etchu, restating our resolve all along the way. Through nine hellish days of heat and rain, all my old maladies tormenting me again, feverish and weak, I could not write.

> Altair meets Vega
> tomorrow—Tanabata—
> already the night is changed

> High over wild seas
> surrounding Sado Island:
> the river of heaven

TODAY WE CAME through places with names like Children-Desert-Parents, Lost Children, Send-Back-the-Dog, and Turn-Back-the-Horse—some of the most fearsomely dangerous places in all the North Country. And well named. Weakened and exhausted, I went to bed early but was roused by the voices of two young women in the room next door. Then an old man's voice joined theirs. They were prostitutes from Niigata in Echigo Province and were on their way to Ise Shrine in the south, the old man seeing them off at this barrier, Ichiburi. He would turn back to Niigata in the morning, carrying their letters home. One girl quoted the *Shinkokinshū* poem, "On the beach where white waves fall, / we all wander like children into every circumstance, / carried forward every day. . . ." And as they bemoaned their fate in life, I fell asleep.

In the morning, preparing to leave, they came to ask directions. "May we follow along behind?" they asked. "We're lost and not a little fearful. Your robes bring the spirit of the Buddha to our journey." They had mistaken us for priests. "Our way includes detours and retreats," I told them. "But follow anyone on this road, and the gods will see you through." I hated to leave them in tears and thought about them hard for a long time after we left. I told Sora, and he wrote down:

> Under one roof, prostitute and priest,
> we all sleep together:
> moon in a field of clover

WE MANAGED TO CROSS all "forty-eight rap-ids" of the Kurobe River on our way to the bay of Nago. Although it was no longer spring, we thought even an autumn visit to the wisteria at Tako—made famous in the *Man'yōshū*—worth the trouble, and asked the way: "Five miles down the coast, then up and over a mountain. A few fishermen's shacks, but no lodging, no place even to camp." It sounded so difficult, we pushed on instead into the province of Kaga.

> Fragrance of ripening rice
> as we pass by
> the angry Ariso Sea

WE CROSSED MOUNT UNOHANA and Kurikara Valley at noon on the fifteenth day of the seventh moon and entered Kanazawa, where we took rooms at an inn with a merchant from Osaka, a Mr. Kasho, who was in town to attend memorial services for the haiku poet Isshō, locally renowned for his verse and devotion to craft. The poet's elder brother served as host, the poet having died last winter.

> Tremble if you can,
> gravemound:
> this autumn wind's my cry

WE WERE INVITED to visit a thatched-roof
hermitage:

> Autumn's very cool
> hands busy peeling
> cucumber and eggplant

Later, written along the road:

> Intense hot red sun
> and this autumn wind
> indifferent

AT A VILLAGE called Komatsu:

> Aptly named Komatsu,
> Little Pine, a breeze blows
> over pampas grass and clover

Here we visited Tada Shrine to see Sanemori's helmet and a piece of his brocade armor-cloth presented to him by Lord Yoshitomo when he served the Genji clan. His helmet was no common soldier's gear: engraved with chrysanthemums and ivy from eyehole to earflap, crowned with a dragon's head between two horns. After Sanemori died on the battlefield, Kiso Yoshinaka sent it with a prayer, hand-carried to the shrine by Higuchi Jirō, Sanemori's friend. The story's inscribed on the shrine.

Ungraciously, under
a great soldier's empty helmet,
a cricket sings

ALONG THE ROAD to Yamanaka Hot Springs, Mount Shirane rose behind our backs. At the foot of a mountain to our left we found a small temple to Kannon, Bodhisattva of Compassion. After the retired Emperor Kazan had made a pilgrimage to the thirty-three western temples, he enshrined an image of the goddess Kannon here, naming the temple Nata, using the first syllables of the first and last temples of the thirty-three: Nachi and Tanigumi. A small thatched-roof temple built on a rock among boulders and twisted pines, Nata lingers in the mind:

> Whiter than the stones
> of White Stone Temple:
> autumn wind blows

WE BATHED in mineral hot springs comparable to those at Ariake.

> After bathing for hours
> in Yamanaka's waters
> I couldn't even pick a flower

Our host at the inn was a young man named Kumenosuke. His father was a knowledgeable haiku poet who had embarrassed the poet Teishitsu of Kyoto when Teishitsu was still ignorant and young. The latter thus returned to Kyoto and apprenticed himself to haiku master Teitoku. When Teishitsu returned to Yamanaka to judge a poetry contest, he refused to accept payment, having been so humbled. It's a legend around here now.

SORA, suffering from persistent stomach ailments, was forced to return to his relatives in Nagashima in Ise Province. His parting words:

> Sick to the bone
> if I should fall
> I'll lie in fields of clover

He carries his pain as he goes, leaving me empty. Like paired geese parting in the clouds.

> Now falling autumn dew
> obliterates my hatband's
> "We are two"

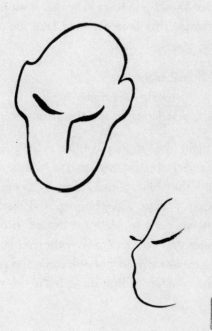

I STAYED AT ZENSHŌ-JI, a temple near the castle town of Daishōji in Kaga Province. It was from this temple that Sora departed here the night before, leaving behind:

> All night long
> listening to autumn winds
> wandering in the mountains

One night like a thousand miles, as the proverb says, and I too listened to fall winds howl around the same temple. But at dawn, the chanting of sutras, gongs ringing, awakened me. An urgent need to leave for distant Echizen Province. As I prepared to leave the temple, two young monks arrived with ink stone and paper in hand. Outside, willow leaves fell in the wind.

> Sweep the garden
> all kindnesses
> falling willow leaves repay

My sandals already on, I wrote it quickly and departed.

At the Echizen province border, at an inlet town called Yoshizaki, I hired a boat and sailed for the famous pines of Shiogoshi. Saigyō wrote:

> All the long night
> salt-winds drive
> storm-tossed waves
> and moonlight drips
> through Shiogoshi pines

This one poem says enough. To add another would be like adding a sixth finger to a hand.

In the town of matsuoka, I visited Tenryū
Temple, renewing an old friendship with the
elder. The poet Hokushi from Kanazawa,
intending only to see me off a way, had come
this far with me, but turned back here. His
poems on views along the way were sensitive,
and I wrote for him:

> Written on my summer fan
> torn in half
> in autumn

WALKED A FEW MILES into the mountains to pray at Dōgen Zenji's temple, Eihei-ji. To have placed it here, "a thousand miles from the capital," as the old saying goes, was no accident.

AFTER SUPPER, I set out for Fukui, five miles down the road, the way made difficult by falling dark. An old recluse named Tōsai lived somewhere around here. More than ten years had passed since he came to visit me in Edo. Was he still alive? I was told he still lived near town, a small, weathered house just off the road, lost in tangles of gourd vines growing under cypress. I found the gate and knocked. A lonely-looking woman answered. "Where do you come from, honorable priest? The master has gone to visit friends." Probably his wife, she looked like she'd stepped right out of *Genji*.

I found Tōsai and stayed two days before deciding to leave to see the full moon at Tsuruga Harbor. Tōsai, enthused, tied up his robes in his sash, and we set off with him serving as guide.

MOUNT SHIRANE FADED behind us and Mount Hina began to appear. We crossed Asamuzu Bridge and saw the legendary "reeds of Tamae" in bloom. We crossed Uguisu Barrier at Yuno-o Pass and passed by the ruins of Hiuchi Castle. On Returning Hill we heard the first wild geese of autumn. We arrived at Tsuruga Harbor on the evening of the fourteenth day of the eighth moon. The harbor moonlight was marvelously bright.

I asked at the inn, "Will we have this view tomorrow night?" The innkeeper said, "Can't guarantee weather in Koshiji. It may be clear, but then again it may turn overcast. It may rain." We drank sake with the innkeeper, then paid a late visit to the Kehi Myōjin Shrine honoring the second-century Emperor Chūai. A great spirituality—moonlight in pines, white sands like a touch of frost. In ancient times Yugyō, the second high priest, himself cleared away the grounds, carried stones, and built drains. To this day, people carry sands to the shrine. "*Yugyō-no-sunamochi*," the innkeeper explained, "Yugyō's sand-bringing."

> Transparent moonlight
> shines over Yugyō's sand
> perfectly white

ON THE FIFTEENTH, just as the innkeeper warned, it rained:

> Harvest moon—
> true North Country weather—
> nothing to view

THE SKY CLEARED the morning of the sixteenth. I sailed to Iro Beach a dozen miles away and gathered several colorful shells with a Mr. Tenya, who provided a box lunch and sake and even invited his servants. Tail winds got us there in a hurry. A few fishermen's shacks dotted the beach, and the tiny Hokke Temple was disheveled. We drank tea and hot sake, lost in a sweeping sense of isolation as dusk came on.

> Loneliness greater
> than *Genji*'s Suma Beach:
> the shores of autumn

> Wave after wave
> mixes tiny shells
> with bush clover flowers

Tosai wrote a record of our afternoon and left it at the temple.

A DISCIPLE, ROTSŪ, had come to Tsuruga to travel with me to Mino Province. We rode horses into the castle town of Ōgaki. Sora returned from Ise, joined by Etsujin, also riding a horse. We gathered at the home of Jokō, a retired samurai. Lord Zensen, the Keikō family men, and other friends arrived by day and night, all to welcome me as though I'd come back from the dead. A wealth of affection!

Still exhausted and weakened from my long journey, on the sixth day of the darkest month, I felt moved to visit Ise Shrine, where a twenty-one-year Rededication Ceremony was about to get under way. At the beach, in the boat, I wrote:

> Clam ripped from its shell
> I move on to Futami Bay:
> passing autumn

Notes

p. 1   "The moon and sun are eternal travelers." This line echoes the famous preface to a poem ("Peach Garden Banquet on a Spring Night") by the T'ang-dynasty poet Li Po.

p. 1   "some who perished along the road." Bashō is thinking of T'ang poet Tu Fu (712–770) and the wandering monk Saigyō (1118–1190).

p. 2   "Even this grass hut / may be transformed / into a doll's house." This image—of Bashō's tiny thatched hut dwarfed by his patron's mansion— refers to Hina Matsuri, the Girls' Festival.

p. 3   "transparent moon still visible." This is an allusion to a line from *The Tale of Genji*.

p. 5   "Go stone skies." Go is an ancient Chinese board game played with black and white pieces called "stones," which create patterns as the game progresses.

p. 6   *Konoshiro* literally means "in-place-of-child," a reference to another legend.

p. 8   Kūkai, also called Kōbō Daishi (774–835), founded the Shingon Buddhist sect. The temple at Nikkō was actually founded by Shōdō (737–817).

p. 9   "his poem is pregnant with meaning." Japanese poets often changed their names, as had Bashō himself. Traveling in Buddhist robes was both safer and in keeping with Bashō's spiritual pilgrimage.

p. 10   "Stopped awhile / inside a waterfall: / the summer begins." This verse refers to Shinto-Buddhist spring ritual bathing.

p. 14   Dog-shooting had been, briefly, in the early Kamakura period, a sport for archers.

p. 14   The story of Lady Tamamo is told in the Noh play *Sesshō-seki*.

p. 14   Yoichi's legendary feat is told in *The Tale of the Heike*.

p. 14   "In summer mountains / bow to holy high

water clogs / bless this long journey." The "high water clogs" refers to the "rain clogs" of En-no-Gyōja, eighth-century founder of the Shugen sect.

p. 15   Bashō studied Zen under Butchō (1643–1715) at Chokei Temple in Edo between 1673 and 1684.

p. 16   Myōzenji and Hōun were Chinese Zen (Ch'an) masters famed for their asceticism.

p. 20   The phrases "autumn winds" and "red maple leaves" refer to poems by Nōin and Yorimasa, both influences on Saigyō.

p. 20   Kiyosuke (1104–1177) was a Heian-period poet.

p. 22   Gyōki (668–749), high priest during the Nara period, was considered a bodhisattva.

p. 23   *Katsumi* echoes the famous cry of "Katsu!" used in Zen.

p. 26   Minamoto Yoshitsune (1159–1189), the military leader for the Genji clan, was celebrated in stories in *The Tale of the Heike* and various Noh plays. Benkei was a follower of Yoshitsune.

p. 29   The story of Lord Sanekata is told in *The Pillow Book of Sei Shonagon*.

p. 33   The *Kokinshū* is a tenth-century imperial anthology of poetry.

p. 33   The Tenjin Shrine honors Sugawara Michizane (835–903), who was exiled in life, then deified as Tenjin, the "god of letters."

p. 44   Ungo Zenji (1583–1659) was a famous monk.

p. 45   *Waka* is the old name for short poems in lines of 5-7-5-7-7 syllables, later called *tanka*.

p. 47   Kembutso was a famous twelfth-century priest whom Saigyō visited in Matsushima.

p. 48   The *Man'yōshū* (*Collection of Ten Thousand Leaves*) is the first imperial anthology of poetry and was compiled in the eighth century.

p. 51   "Kanefusa's / own white hair / seen in blossoming briar." Kanefusa (1127–1189), although old, fought beside Yoshitsune.

p. 60   Here, Bashō mentions Sennin, Hall of Immortals, almost as a prayer for longevity.

p. 61   "The winds that blow / through South Valley Temple / are sweetened by snow." In the *Li Chi*, the Confucian *Book of Rites*, "a sweet wind from the south" indicates warmth and clarity.

p. 65   Gyōson Sōjō was a twelfth-century poet-priest whose work Bashō read in the *Kinyōshū*.

p. 70   "Mount Chōkai holding up the heavens inverted on the water." This image alludes to famous poems by Wang Wei and Tu Fu.

p. 73   "Altair meets Vega / tomorrow—Tanabata— / already the night is changed." Tanabata Matsuri celebrates the annual romantic reunion of lovers separated all but one night per year, when they cross a bridge of magpies on the seventh night of the seventh month. See also *The Diary of Izumi Shikibu* for more commentary.

p. 73   "High over wild seas / surrounding Sado Island: / the river of heaven." Sado Island was home of political exiles. The "river of heaven" is the Milky Way.

p. 74   The *Shinkokinshū* is the eighth imperial anthology of "new and old poems," and the primary source for Bashō's study of Saigyō's poetry.

p. 80   Sanemori's story is told in *The Tale of the Heike* and in a Noh play by Zeami.

p. 83   Teitoku (1571–1653) was a Kyoto haiku and *renga* scholar and poet.

p. 84   "Like paired geese parting in the clouds" recalls a poem of Bashō's written while still in his teens following the death of his lord, Yoshitada; it also carries echoes of Tu Fu.

p. 84   "Now falling autumn dew / obliterates my hatband's / 'We are two.'" It was a custom for travelers to wear inscribed hatbands saying that they traveled "with the Buddha," thereby reducing risks.

p. 88   "To add another would be like adding a sixth finger to a hand." This image is derived from *Chuang Tzu*, chapter 8.

p. 90   Dōgen (1200–1253) was the founder of the Sōtō Zen sect.

p. 97   Ise is Japan's principal Shinto shrine.

SHAMBHALA CENTAUR EDITIONS are named for a classical modern typeface designed by the eminent American typographer Bruce Rogers. Modeled on a fifteenth-century Roman type, Centaur was originally an exclusive titling font for the Metropolitan Museum of Art, New York. The first book in which it appeared was Maurice de Guérin's *The Centaur*, printed in 1915.

Until recently, Centaur type was available only for handset books printed on letterpress. Its elegance and clarity make it the typeface of choice for Shambhala Centaur Editions, which include outstanding classics of the world's literary and spiritual traditions.